Don't Forget!

Mother's Day

Monica Hughes

Heinemann
LIBRARY

www.heinemann.co.uk/library

Visit our website to find out more information about **Heinemann Library** books.

To order:
- ☎ Phone 44 (0) 1865 888066
- 🗎 Send a fax to 44 (0) 1865 314091
- 💻 Visit the Heinemann Bookshop at www.heinemann.co.uk/library to browse our catalogue and order online.

First published in Great Britain by Heinemann Library, Halley Court, Jordan Hill, Oxford OX2 8EJ, a division of Reed Educational and Professional Publishing Ltd. Heinemann is a registered trademark of Reed Educational and Professional Publishing Ltd.

OXFORD MELBOURNE AUCKLAND JOHANNESBURG BLANTYRE
GABORONE IBADAN PORTSMOUTH NH (USA) CHICAGO

Designed by Joanna Sapwell and StoryBooks
Originated by Ambassador Litho Ltd
Printed by Wing King Tong, Hong Kong, China

ISBN 0 431 15404X
06 05 04 03 02
10 9 8 7 6 5 4 3 2 1

British Library Cataloguing in Publication Data
Hughes, Monica
    Mother's Day. – (Don't Forget)
    1. Mother's Day – Juvenile literature
    I.Title
    394 . 2'62

Acknowledgements
The Publishers would like to thank the following for permission to reproduce photographs: AKG London pp. 6, 24; Bridgeman Art Library p. 10; Collections/Jarrold Publishing p. 18; Corbis pp. 8, 16, 27; Corbis/Richard Radstone p. 25; Corbis/Adam Woolfitt p. 9; Corbis/Francis Reiss p. 14; Corbis/Jonathan Blair p. 7; Corbis/Joseph Sohm p. 17, 26; Corbis/Laura Dwight p. 4; Corbis/Lindsay Hebberd p. 29; Food Features p. 12; Garden Picture Library p. 13; Getty Images p. 28; Getty Images Stone p. 5; Holt International p. 19; Hulton Getty p. 15; Topham/Photri p. 27; Topham Picturepoint p. 11; Trevor Clifford pp. 20, 21, 22, 23.

Cover photograph reproduced with permission of Trevor Clifford.

Our thanks to Stuart Copeman for his assistance in the preparation of this book.

Every effort has been made to contact copyright holders of any material reproduced in this book. Any omissions will be rectified in subsequent printings if notice is given to the Publishers.

Contents

Words printed in bold letters, **like this**, are explained in the Glossary.

What is Mother's Day?

Mother's Day is a special time to think about, and say 'thank you' to, mothers everywhere. In Britain it is held on the fourth Sunday in **Lent**, which is in March or April. It is held on a different day in some other countries.

At one time, the day was known as 'Mothering Sunday' but now it is more usually known as Mother's Day. It is a day set aside to give mothers a special treat. The day often begins with breakfast in bed and most mothers have a rest from their normal work. The rest of the family might have a special Sunday lunch.

A mother and daughter enjoying reading together

Special cards are sent for Mother's Day and many of these are made by children. Shops sell chocolates, flowers and other Mother's Day presents, but many children also make their own gifts.

Flowers for mother on Mother's Day

What do you call your mother?

There are lots of different words in English for mother including mummy, mum, mom, ma and mamma. In many languages the word for mother often begins with the sound 'mmm', for example *mére* (French), *mutter* (German), *maji* (**Hindi**) and *umee* (Urdu). This may be because this is one of the first sounds a young baby can say.

5

When was the first Mother's Day?

The **custom** of a special time to remember mothers goes back to ancient spring festivals, thousands of years ago. It has not always been called Mother's Day.

In ancient Greece there was a spring festival to celebrate mothers. It was in **honour** of the goddess Rhea, the mother of all gods. Rhea was the wife of Cronus, the god of time.

Ancient sculpture of Rhea and Cronus

In ancient Rome there was a festival of *Hilaria*. This festival was in honour of the goddess Cybele, the mother of all the gods.

Hilaria was held on 25 March, the first day after the spring **equinox**. This is a time, which happens twice a year, when night and day are the same length. Lots of games were played and there was also a solemn procession in which a statue of Cybele was carried through the streets.

Roman sculpture of a mother and baby

More celebrations

There was another Roman festival in celebration of mothers called *Matronali*. There were feasts, dancing and games in the streets. From the word *'Matronali'* we get the word 'matron'. As well as meaning a head nurse or housekeeper, matron also means mother.

 # The first Mothering Sunday

From the **Middle Ages** the Christian Church has set aside a special day to remember mothers. This was the middle Sunday of **Lent**. The Virgin Mary, the mother of Jesus was celebrated on the earliest Mothering Sundays. People made a special visit to the church and brought offerings to the Virgin Mary.

The 'Mother Church' was also important on Mothering Sunday. Many villages were too small or too poor to have their own church and so several villages shared a large 'Mother Church', some distance away.

Oil painting of Mary and Jesus from the 19th century

St Peter's Church, Lewtrenchard, Dartmoor

On Mothering Sunday people went back to the Mother Church where they may have been **baptized**. Sometimes people from the larger churches went to visit the nearest **cathedral** on Mothering Sunday.

What else did people do?

In some places an old **custom** known as 'clypping the church' was held on Mothering Sunday. Clypping means greeting or **honouring**. On Mothering Sunday all the **parishioners** walked round the church holding hands and singing a hymn. This was meant to show love for the **parish**.

What is 'going a-mothering'?

Mothering Sunday also used to be known as 'Refreshment Sunday'. It let people take a break from **fasting**. It was the only time when feasting and games were allowed out of the 40 days of **Lent**. It was a day when families got together. By the 16th century there are records of celebrations of children and grandchildren coming home to the family for a feast.

By the 18th and 19th centuries many children lived away from home as servants in the houses of the wealthy. Servants had one day off a year and were encouraged to 'go a-mothering' – to go home and see their families.

A painting from 1567 of William Brook and his family

Working children being paid before their annual holiday

They would often take a present. This could be money or a **posy** of spring flowers and sometimes something to eat like a 'mothering cake'. There would be a celebration meal, often of lamb or **veal**, and a drink called 'furmety' would be served. This was made of wheat grains boiled in milk, sweetened with sugar and flavoured with a spice called cinnamon.

Other names for Mothering Sunday

At one time, in Scotland and northern England, Mothering Sunday was known as 'Carling Sunday'. Carlings were pancakes made of dried peas that had been soaked and then fried in butter with salt and pepper.

What is a mothering cake?

Children going home for Mothering Sunday would often take with them a 'mothering cake'. This was a cake specially baked for their mothers. Although it was given on Mothering Sunday it would often be saved and eaten on Easter Sunday, at the end of **Lent**.

A mothering cake was usually a cake called a 'simnel cake'. Simnel cake was usually a very rich fruitcake that was boiled in water, before being baked in an oven. Some were made with flour coloured with a yellow spice called saffron. They often had almond icing, called marzipan, on the top. Others were like a Christmas cake with a layer of almond paste in the middle. There were also flat ones, shaped like a saucer and stuffed with currants and almonds.

A simnel cake ready for a Mother's Day tea party

12

Today, simnel cakes are fruitcakes with marzipan in the middle and on the top. There are often small balls or eggs of marzipan on the top and a yellow ribbon tied round the sides.

A basket of **posies**

How did simnel cake get its name?

The simnel cake may take its name from *similia*. This was a type of flour used in ancient Rome. It was a very fine flour and was used in special cakes that were eaten at the spring festival.

Another story is that it was named after two people called Simon and Nell who argued about the best way to cook the cake – should it be boiled or baked in the oven? They agreed to do both and so made a cake sharing both their names. Which of these ideas do you like best?

13

How did Mothering Sunday become Mother's Day?

By the First World War Mothering Sunday was being celebrated less and less. This was partly because workers had more holidays so families could meet together more regularly. By the Second World War Mothering Sunday had been almost forgotten.

The idea of a special day for mothers was **revived** when American soldiers came to Britain during the Second World War. They brought with them the traditions of the American Mother's Day. These traditions included sending cards, giving presents and flowers to mothers on their special day.

American soldiers in Britain in 1945

After the war had ended the new name of Mother's Day was used in Britain. Mothering Sunday was originally a celebration connected to religion and the Christian Church. The modern British Mother's Day has become much more about the family and actual mothers. It is celebrated by people of many **faiths** and is not just a Christian celebration.

A surprise for mother on Mother's Day in 1955

A modern Mother's Day

Children like to give Mother's Day cards and flowers, but what if your mother is away and you cannot see her? E-mail and the Internet now mean you can send your mother an 'e-card' to let her know you are thinking of her on Mother's Day. You could send her a special message by e-mail.

How did Mother's Day start in the USA?

Anna Jarvis aged 43

In 1872 Julia Ward Howe, who lived in the USA, suggested a special day for mothers.

The idea was finally started in 1907 by Anna Jarvis. She began a **campaign** to have a national Mother's Day. Anna's mother, Mrs Anna Reese Jarvis taught at **Sunday school** in the **Methodist Church** in Graftan, West Virginia.

When her mother died, Anna persuaded her mother's church to celebrate a Mother's Day on the second **anniversary** of her death. It was the second Sunday in May. Anna Jarvis and her friends wrote to ministers, businessmen and politicians asking them to support a national Mother's Day.

The American flag flying outside a house on Mother's Day

By 1911 Mother's Day was celebrated in almost every state in America. In 1914, President Woodrow Wilson announced that Mother's Day would be a national holiday and that it would be held on the second Sunday in May.

A flag for Mother's Day

In 1914, the President of the USA announced that the national flag would be displayed on government buildings and at people's homes on Mother's Day as 'a public expression of our love and **reverence** for the mothers of our country'.

Why do we give flowers on Mother's Day?

Today, Mother's Day is a very busy time for **florists**. The most popular flowers given as a present for Mother's Day are spring flowers including daffodils, tulips and violets. The florist arranges flowers in baskets and bouquets. Flowers can be very expensive on the days just before Mother's Day and many people prefer a bunch of flowers picked from the garden.

Children giving their mothers flowers in church on Mothering Sunday

Flowers for Mother's Day

Anna Jarvis's mother's favourite flower was the white carnation. Anna gave these to her friends in memory of her mother on the first **anniversary** of her death. After this people in the USA began wearing carnations on Mother's Day in **honour** of mothers. People like Anna Jarvis, who were remembering a mother who had died, wore white carnations. People whose mothers were alive wore red carnations. Mothers that had had a child who had died wore yellow carnations.

Mothering Sunday in church

Many churches in Britain still celebrate Mothering Sunday with flowers. Small **posies** of flowers like daffodils and violets are given to children in the **congregation**. The children then present the flowers to their mothers.

Mother's Day cards

The first Mother's Day cards were ordinary greeting cards that could be used for any occasion. It wasn't until about 1915 that the words Mother's Day appeared on the cards. Many of the earliest cards had pictures of mothers cooking and cleaning or resting after doing all the housework.

Mother's Day cards have changed over the years. The pictures now show the different lives of mother's today. The messages inside the cards have changed little over the years – they still show just how much mothers are loved and **appreciated**.

There are even cards with greetings to 'An auntie on Mother's Day', 'To the mother of a friend' and even 'For my husband's mother'.

A collection of Mother's Day cards

Mother's Day cards are even better when you make them

Not all Mother's Day cards are bought. Every year, thousands of children make their own Mother's Day cards. These are made with great love and care and often treasured by mothers long after their children have grown up and left home.

A poem for Mother's Day by Howard Johnson

'M' is for the million things she gave me
'O' means only that's she's growing old
'T' is for the tears she shed to save me
'H' is for her heart of purest gold
'E' is for her eyes, with love-light shining
'R' means right and right she'll always be,
Put them all together, they spell
'MOTHER'
A word that means the world to me.

Mother's Day presents

Many people like to give their mother a special present on Mother's Day. Flowers are very popular presents, so are chocolates or perfume. Shop windows often have special displays of suitable presents for Mother's Day.

Some people are worried that the real meaning of the day is lost if an expensive present is needed to show how much a mother is **appreciated**.

Today, there are many special Mother's Day presents

A present for Mother's Day doesn't have to cost anything. On this special day, it is the thought behind the present that counts. Presents that you have made yourself are often the nicest.

Beautiful presents made by you

You could make a woven basket and fill it with homemade sweets. You could sew a needle case or make a bag filled with lavender.

Some children give a present in the form of a promise – perhaps to do something for their mother, like washing-up or some other helpful job.

What do flowers mean?

Flowers are traditionally given as presents on Mother's Day. Some flowers have special meanings:

Daffodils – regards

Bluebells – **constancy**

Lilies of the valley – happiness

Violets – **modesty**

23

How have the lives of mothers changed?

In the past, when a woman got married and had children she did not work outside the home. Her husband went out to work and she stayed at home. It was her full-time job to look after the home and family. Many families were large, with six or seven children being quite common. A few mothers did have help with the cooking, cleaning and looking after their children, but many did not. For many mothers life was very hard work.

Family photograph from about 1895

Today many women go out to work as well as being a mother. If your mum goes out to work, what job does she do? Most families are much smaller than they were in the past and may only have one or two children. Also, today there are machines that make cleaning, washing and cooking much easier.

A modern family

Some women live alone with their children and have to do everything for the family. Most mothers lead very busy lives and it is good that they have at least one day a year when a fuss can be made of them.

Who looks after you?

Today, it is not just mothers who stay at home and look after the children. In some families, the father stays at home while the mother goes out to work. Or they share looking after the family.

All kinds of mothers

On Mother's Day, most people think especially about their real mother (**birth mother**) but these are not the only mothers who are special. A child who has been **adopted** will celebrate Mother's Day with their new mother. Even if a child is not related to their new mother they can still be a happy and loving family.

Some children live with a **foster** family. Their birth parents may not have been able to care or provide for them properly. The foster mother will love and care for her foster children in the same way as birth mothers do.

A **stepmother** is also special on Mother's Day. She may not be a child's blood relative but she will love and care for her stepchild as if she were.

An adopted child having fun with her mother

Mothers can be young or old

It does not really matter whether your mother is your real mother, a foster mother, stepmother or adopted mother. She will still love you, and enjoy special treats, like a card or a present, on Mother's Day.

Famous mothers

Mother Teresa was born on 27 August 1910, in Skopje, Macedonia and died 5 September 1997. She was famous for her **missionary** work helping the sick and poor in Calcutta in India. She is called 'Mother' because she was the leader of a special group of nuns.

The Queen Mother was born on 4 August 1900, and died on 30 March 2002. She lived for over a hundred years. She was the mother of our Queen, Elizabeth II.

Mother's Day around the world

Mother's Day celebrations take place all over the world but they are not always held on the same day. For instance, in the USA and Canada Mother's Day is celebrated on the second Sunday in May. Denmark, Finland, Italy, Turkey, Australia, Japan and Belgium also celebrate Mother's Day on this day.

In France, Mother's Day is celebrated on the last Sunday in May. It is treated rather like a family birthday. Everyone in the family gathers for a special meal. This might be at home or in a restaurant. At the end of the meal the mother is presented with a beautiful cake.

A Mother's Day barbecue

In Sweden Mother's Day is also on the last Sunday in May and is a family holiday. The Swedish Red Cross sells small plastic flowers on the days leading up to Mother's Day. The money raised from these 'Mother's Flowers' are used to help needy mothers and their children.

In Spain and Portugal Mother's day is celebrated on 8 December. It is closely linked to the church, especially to Mary, the mother of Jesus.

An Indian mother and her child

An Indian celebration

In India there is a ten-day **Hindu** festival called *Durga Puja* held in early October. The festival **honours** Durga, the 'Divine Mother'. She is the most important of all Hindu goddesses.

 # Glossary

adopted   legally made a member of a new family

anniversary   same date as something that happened in the past

appreciated   valued and enjoyed

baptized   water placed on a person as a sign of joining the Christian faith

birth mother   woman who gave birth to the child

campaign   organized action to achieve something

cathedral   larger or important church

congregation   people worshipping together

constancy   never changing

customs   usual ways of doing something

eqinox   a day, twice a year, when night and day are the same length

faiths   religions

fasting   going without food

florists   people who sell flowers

foster   when someone looks after a child as if they were its parent

Hindus (**Hindi**)   people who follow the Hindu religion. Hindi means to do with the Hindu faith.

honour   give praise and respect

Lent   period of 40 days before the Christian celebration of Easter

Methodist Church Christian church founded by
John Wesley

Middle Ages period of time from AD 1000 to AD 1400

missionary someone sent to another country to spread
their faith

modesty not boastful or showy

parish area with its own church

parishioners people belonging to a parish

posy (**posies**) small bunch of flowers

reverence respect and admiration

revived brought back into use

stepmother woman who is not your mother but is
married to your father

Sunday school meeting for children linked to a
Christian service

veal meat from a calf

Index

Titles in the *Don't Forget* series:

Hardback   0 431 15401 5

Hardback   0 431 15403 1

Hardback   0 431 15405 8

Hardback   0 431 15400 7

Hardback   0 431 15404 X

Hardback   0 431 15402 3

Find out about other Heinemann titles on our website www.heinemann.co.uk/library